Leaving Death Row

Leaving Death Row

By

Reginald Sinclair Lewis

ISBN: 1-58721-677-9

1stBooks – rev. 6/16/00

ACKNOWLEDGEMENTS PAGE

"Black wings" was published in <u>African American Review.,</u> Volume 33, Number 1, 1999

"Autumn Dawn" was published in <u>Bitterroot.</u> Copyright © 1991, Volume xxx, No. 100.

"Will I Ever See You Again?" was first published in <u>Huh?</u> Magazine. Copyright © 1991.

"Releasing The Chains" was first published in <u>Poetry:</u> USA. Copyright © 1990.

"For James Baldwin" was first published in <u>Poetry</u>: USA. Copyright © 1990.

"Who Knows?" was first published in <u>Lifelines.</u> Copyright © 1990, No. 50. In the same issue, "Releasing The Chains" republished with permission of the author.

"Domestic Violence" was published in <u>Axis,</u> formerly <u>Sun/Father</u> Journal. Copyright © 1990, No. 4.

"Let's Get Married" was first published in <u>Talk of the World</u> Magazine. Copyright © 1989.

Poems "Whispers", "Brown Eyes", "One Day Soon" and "Whisper I'm Gone" all appeared first in <u>The Philadelphia Tribune</u>, on a weekly basis, in "Poet's Corner." Copyright © 1985.

"In The Big Yard" was first published in <u>Fortune News</u>. Copyright © 1989.

"In The Big Yard" was republished in <u>Poetry:</u> USA, with permission of the author. Copyright © 1990.

"The Way I See Him", appeared in <u>The Other Side</u>, September-December 1997.

"Wanna Go Home", and "In The Big Yard", were reprinted in <u>Word Wrights!</u> No. 11, Fall/Winter 1997.

"Queens Rise" (For the Women on Death Row), was published in <u>Women on the Row,</u> Volume 1, Issue 6, January 1999.

"Shaniqua is Pregnant" and "Johnny's A Painter", appeared in <u>The Exchange,</u> No. 9, 1999.

"In The Big Yard", by this Poet's permission, was published in <u>Doing Time, 25 Years of Prison Writing,</u> PGS 54-55, <u>Arcade Publishing</u>, New York, 1999.

"Kissing Josephine", will have appeared in <u>Pearl</u>, November 1999 Issue.

HONORS AND AWARDS

First prize, poetry, for "In The Big Yard," P.E.N. American Center 1988 Writing Awards for Prisoners. 568 Broadway, New York, NY 10012.

Third Prize, short story, "Sweeter Than Sugar," P.E.N. American Center, Writing Awards for Prisoners, 1987.

Honorable mention, "Best of Rhyme Time," 1988.

Certificate of award, for "Brown Eyes," March 22, 1988. Hutton Publications.

Certificate of award, for "Illusions," June 8, 1988. Hutton Publications.

Certificate of award, for "Milestones," August 22, 1988. Hutton Publications.

3rd Place, Drama category, for Good Night, Boo Baby, 1999 Pen Prison Writing Awards.

Contents

PRELUDE

(For <u>Leaving Death Row</u>)

<u>By</u>

Reginald Sinclair Lewis

The questions are always posed by strangers, remote readers, and even my own friends: <u>When did you begin writing? How did you ever learn to write so well, Reggie?</u>

The answers are never so simple to proffer because the questions come after they have read or reread a single poem or a series of poems that had become their favorite, poems demanding explanations about its conception, composition, and inspiration. The <u>When</u> is easy enough to pinpoint but the <u>How</u> is attributable to any number of reasons. Few poets can account for those internal cosmic beings who commands the muse., answerable only to the invisible essence of time.

My radio sitting atop my desk blares out Jazz. I usually write while listening to those baad ass old Cats--Coltrane. Miles. Dizzy. Yardbird.

And the smooth, sultry Lady Balladeers, all smoke and fire. Any one of their cuts could've inspired the rhythmic sycopation that ebbs and flows through my more Jazzy poems.

And it could've been something I'd seen on TV--stark images emblazoned in the reservoirs of my mind-- a gallant black olympic athlete streaking past hapless opponents and into the annals of History; A Police beatdown of an innocent Black suspect and the Southcentral L.A. riots; serial killings; some Ghetto Black girl getting raped, impregnated; Kids stomping, Marchin' to Death Row--some dusty Old Con taking his last breath, conjures inspiration.

It is the <u>When</u> question that evokes clarity of the moment that precipitated the heady burst of creativity.

It was August 13, 1983. Sweat poured profusely down my brown face as I stared at the twelve white members of the jury.

Cold Pale faces glared back. "How do you find the Defendant?" The Judge asked them. "Guilty, your Honor", the Jury Foreman said." We Sentence him to Death". I sank in my chair, I was only 20-Something then. <u>Death?</u>

I moved about sluggishly, as if in a dream. My Mama wept inconsolably. The Prisoners stared in awe from a distance. <u>Damn, Homie. You got the Death Penalty?</u> their eyes seemed to say. But I was too proud to cry. The thought of being executed weighed heavily on my mind--and I slept for two long days.

I rose with the clear awakening of my own fragile mortality. How fleeting life is. But there was something about being trapped in a deep dark hole that makes you keep clawing your way back up--even if you'll never make it.

I refused to allow a jury's erroneous verdict to define me. I knew I was not--and will <u>never</u> be--the sum total equaling a mere Death Row Inmate, a number corralled, stored, locked away and forgotten. I became fiercely determined to break the interminable cycle of boredom and loneliness and the implacable resolute despair that induces a gradual descent into madness.

I immersed myself in the books by the Black Harlem Renaissance writers: Richard Wright. Langston Hughes. Zora Neale Hurston. James Baldwin. Ralph Ellison, and so many others.

In the enforced solitude, reading burgeoned my consciousness, ignited sparks in the pit of my gut and raced through my bloodstream like wild brush fires. <u>This is what led to my self-discovery as a writer.</u> This is the answer to the <u>How in the world did you learn to write like that?</u>

I write every day. I rewrite. Cut. Polish. The blank white canvas of the page became creations filled with spectacular colors, images, sounds, and living, breathing beings. From the lowest depths of Human Misery flowed the sweetest testament of dreams.

They are the poems in this book, poems that garnered Awards and Honorable mentions and certificates of merit.

<u>Leaving Death Row</u> is my florid, ever- unfurling dream, my winged chariot of imagination and memories escaping this low-

slung mass of steel and stone and bullit-proof glass that seeks to imprison their flight.

WANNA GO HOME

Heading on across the border
Past dead cities fading in the hazy
Dawn, the brown dust swirls, high like ghosts.
Been so long since I sat at Momma's
Kitchen table,
Sizzling with hot buttered biscuits, deep
Fried chicken, and slippery chocolate cake.
Oh, I want to go back. Back,
Big and strong now, yet
Still a sweet little boy in
Momma's weary melancholy eyes.
And now that I think about her…
I wanna go home.
Last time I saw the fellas
We were hanging out on the corner.
It was summertime and we were talking
Loud about nothin',
Passing round the smudged, long-necked
Bottle of cold wine,
And watchin' the girls float by.
They're long gone now, most of them,
My cool gang, and now that I think
About them…
I wanna go home.
Back to Philly, my hometown,
The tall tenements swaying dreamy under
The dark urban sky,
Where fat Italian mothers
Lean on the sill of bedroom windows,
Seeing nothing.
Voices cutting across the grit
Of the day--it's the impossible
Noise from the city--Super Sundays
And Eagle games. Homeboy Grover Washington's
Horn blowing down the long cool alleys

At jazz concerts in Fairmount Park,
Where vendors shrill crazy--getting
Rich selling hot dogs and sodas and
Soft pretzels--coins jingling joyously
As slick sugar daddies cruise along
Kelly Drive in big shiny Cadillacs
Under the twinkling stars,
The top down,
Passing pretty rainbow girls, blowing kisses, and
Singing wild and passionate songs.

IN THE BIG YARD

Rumors abound Inmate so-and-so done gotta parole date.
Last Monday, but sucker don't even
Know his woman done run off with "Sweet Cadillac Willie"
Who spent her
    Welfare check on gasoline an' blow on a new pair of skins.
An' that scary lil wimp locks on B-Block ain't cool, man.
Snitched on his rap-partner 'bout that rape-kidnap-homicide-robbery back in '76.
Hit goin' down in the Big Yard.
    Stay away, Homie.
'Cause bookies layin' ten-to-one odds some lieutenant finds the rat with his
Head propped up on the
    End of a long shank.
When they find the body what they do is ship it home in a cheap plywood box,
Tag with his number on it swinging listlessly on his big toe an' a
"What
Have I done to deserve this?" look on his dumb ugly face.
Other day seen new blood shambling through
    The reception gate talking' loud an' all cocky like he Mr. T.
So a
Big mean lookin' con doin' life for
    Mutilating his pregnant wife walks boldly up to Young blood an'
Whispers somethin' soft an' sweet to 'im an' next day Young blood's lips are
Red an' glossy an'
    His hair is long an' straight an' he's switchin' 'round the big Yard
Like he Diana Ross.
'An the big con says, "Hot young punk for sale, y'all!"
Squinting into the sun, Old Man "Pops" says he been down so long he done lost
Count.

"Kinda git used to it af-ta while, son", Pops says: "The big time hoods an'
Their paper Cadillacs on cruise control.
The Ho's on the stroll down the endless lightless white-clay strip.
Crack junkies chillin' out on smoke-marshmallow clouds.
Pseudo-intellectuals over there rappin' 'bout the struggle.
An' the hapless chorus of crooners tryin' to sound like the Temptations."
    Pops says he don't pay 'im
    No mind an' he ain't listenin'
Don't even care 'bout nothing' 'cause he ain't neva had a woman noway.
Old bones runs the Big Yard through
    Chugging along like a locomotive that neva stops.
Runs all day long--
Bookies layin' ten-to-one odds old Pops plannin' to fly right over the big Wall.

RELEASING THE CHAINS
(FOR PAULA COOPER)

I've known so many young black girls
Like you--the daughters of Malcolm
And Martin and Mandela.
The chains wound taut around
Your wrist fetters your wings--
And you cannot fly--
Brown bird of Paradise.
The tall dark-haired preppy strangles
A young woman in Central Park--
Gets his face on the cover of *People*.
Yet, in the slatted darkness
Of your cell you can barely
See the light of the moon.
Filtering hauntingly through
The cold space between the bars.
Ghost-shadows cloud the symmetry
Of your caramel-colored face,
The prominent roundness of your hips--
Held captive by the black-robed
Gestapo's seeking to exterminate
Children by lawless decree.
Oh, Paula, what will happen to all
Your springs? What will become
Of your sweet adolescent dreams? And
The exotic rainbow in your smile?
Yeah, and those adoring praline eyes,
Those diaphanous pools that
The world fell through--
That the universe danced to--
The delicate rhythm of your heartbeat.
And all those civilized countries
That chimed--"We love you, Paula.
We forgive."--
During those long grueling hours

Of your despair.
Even the Pope sang your praise--
Releasing the chains

WHO KNOWS?

Maybe I'll write a movie in Hollywood.
Perhaps a classic American novel.
Lyrics for songs.
Maybe even a Broadway play.
Or a book of prize-winning poems.
Maybe I'll even write about me.
Maybe I'll get around to doing
All those things. You'll see.
Maybe I'll die before I do anything.
Who knows?

JUST ANOTHER DAY

At first light a perfunctory
Dawn unfurls over
A million red bricks in the
Ancient wall--
And the stone face keeper arrives,
Performs an indelicate task.
He leans, grunts, picks his nose--
Shoves a battered tray
Of inedible slush through the bars.
Hot steam rises from the morning coffee
Like sinuous cobras.
What day is it?
He hurries away.
I wish I could escape this place.
I should have left long time ago.
There are hours of waiting.
The sleep that never comes
Flicking the channel.
Damn!
Ain't nothing on the TV but reruns.
Maybe I'll read a good book
To pass the time.
Do push-ups. Jumping jacks.
Cheat at solitaire.
The enforced stillness,
The bleeding light
Poems speak in whispers.
Afternoon spent pacing the floor
In mincing strides--back and forth
Back and forth--
Climbing the sky till I reach the moon,
Arms swinging, nerves wound taut
Around shooting stars,
Slicing through the morass
Of electric eons,

Light years, shunted.
Thunder burst against smoke-storms
And varicose veins hot-crimson,
Roiling,
My brain throbbing, about to explode.
A hand juts out--
It's the warden--twisting the dagger.
And cannibals feast on the blood and the
Meat of the soul.
I don't want to die here.
I want to know about all the things
I've missed. Places. Spaces. Faces.
Blood is not sweeter than jailhouse wine.
All those experiences I
Saw dissipating in the night-dust
Swirling up from the floor--
Over the urine-stained walls of doom,
And the demons of my private agony, descending,
Where I am held hostage,
Trapped, like an eagle,
In this impassable quandary of
Infinite boredom, isolated from this
Tragic reality.
Will I ever leave this place?
They told me last year
But they never came.
And the tears never come, they never
Do, stubborn me, I laughed.
Indicted for being a man?
Indicted for being a black man!
If I close my eyes I can see the music
If I close my eyes you may
Never see me again.
I'm closing my eyes. Not to sleep but
To envision the women--
Sleek. Beautiful. Sun-kissed.
In skimpy bikinis, exotic headdress and
Bright print garb.

The women puttering about the beach
And lying on the hot coral sand,
Beyond them tall ships chug across
The calm turquoise glaze,
Past the shaggy-tipped palms
Swaying above me in the
Soft, balmy breeze. Yeah…
Jolted awake!
I am sprawled on my bunk, veering
Back from the reveries.
The bell tolled at midnight.

LEAVING DEATH ROW

Fifteen years from home and I'm maxed out.
My stuff's all packed. Boxes bulge with
Tattered legal briefs and lost appeals,
Stacks of tear-stained letters and the collection
Of haunting photographs of old girlfriends.
Can't leave without hollerin' at the homies.
The brother with no TV gets my portable zenith.
The aspiring young rapper earned my radio.
The George Jackson wanna-be needs my books.
And even though the old con downstairs
Ain't got but one leg left--
Let him have my scruffy old shoes.
Because where I'm going I won't be needing them.
I went out like this and winged back
Plenty of times--
From the lush landscapes of day dreams,
The deep blue infinity of madness,
All the way from the last-minute reprieve
Of the executioner's potion--
One way or the other--
I'm leaving death row.

BLACK WINGS

(For Michael Johnson, Olympic Champion--1996)

In your blazing evolutionary flight
to eternal greatness--God had to have
cut you from a big BAAAD cat--
perhaps a strain of
graceful Afrikan gazelles--or a fleet
of pink swans streaking through paradise.
You was smokin', Homie.
Sizzling.
Gone.
Run, boy! Yo' mama's callin' ya!
Your long sleek legs striding through your
dream--galloping over continents and
oceans and riverine plains--
you never once looked back, not even when
the stars and the sun
and monsoon moons prostrated themselves
at your gold sneakered feet.
How did you race past the wind--
past Odin feasting on the souls of
long-dead heroes?

WHERE ARE YOU NOW?
(FOR AUNT MARIAN)

With only six months left you insisted the cancer was nothing.

Long after the surgeon mutilated your breast, the stones chipped
away, like wind erosion.

And when the chemo took your luxurious red hair you didn't
even panic,

Or cry the blues.

Your dignity intact, swathed your wound with a replica of long,
dense curls

Once beautifully yours.

"It'll come back," you said

And like you, it never did.

And they were there in prayers,

Your hours of wake and fitful sleep,

Even in those fleeting moments of hearty, rambunctious
laughter, the renascent

Interludes of hopeful remission.

They were there when the beast coveted you, when it

Tossed you about like a stuffed rag doll,

Knowing full well it wouldn't go away.

And the medications you refused to take, saying the painkillers
made you sick,

While that awful machine made you look like a fat elephant.

And then you were difficult to hold,

A fighter, beating back the searing pain.

Your tortured soul imprisoned in a miasma of gray-shark agony.

They said that you were incontinent,

That there was nothing left in your eyes but emptiness,

A fathomless, queerlike glaze.

And then all of a sudden something rose from the abysmal beast
and you were

Raging against it, cursing it, but not God: "Go away! Leave me
alone!"

And then you were wrestling with it--even laughing in its cruel,
ugly face.

Someone screamed!
But it wasn't you.
Because you didn't even mention the loan, the twenty dollars, so
I could enter
That poetry contest,
I need to repay you as much as I needed to win. Remembering
that I was
Terrified of losing,
Your pillars holding up my faith.
"Don't worry, Boo, Baby. You'll win," you said.
But I never did.
What shall I do now?
I still have your photographs,
The treasured memories,
When you were so much more beautiful.
You mailed them to me before your tragic denouement.
Enclosed them in your long, sweet letters, daintily perfumed
with kindred,
Preternatural love.
"Remember me, always," you wrote.
As if you thought I would forget.
I'm looking at your face. Ah, royalty!
Mute and queenly, your composure,
Stilled against the timeless depths of wondrous light, etched in
snow frosted
Frames, which capture the very essence of you.
You, at home, at work, at church,
Even at the beach.
Your soft, round face radiant under the golden sunlight,
Or luminescent under the silk-white moon, wild and persimmon
behind the
Glowing bottled candlelight,
In an exquisite restaurant of your choice.
Where are you now?
I need to know--the signs in the Favonian wind.
With wandering eyes I'm searching for you, beyond the orange-
red sunset, in

Journeys to Utopia, deep way down in the hidden crevices of the
    earth, and
Even in the billowing fragrance,
Seeping from the wild, crimson rose.
Perhaps the gods were kind to sprinkle the crystal dust of your
    soul amid the
Crumbled ruins in the ancient city of Acropolis;
Would you, someday, majestically rise, like tall, marble beams
    against a
Cobalt-blue sky?
"Oh, don't be silly, Boo, Baby," you would say. As if I were
    still your pesty
Little dreamer.
I wasn't there when you left. But it was the dead of winter, they
    recall, a
Sad, gray, miserable day. You gave it all up, let it all go,
Your eyelids fluttering like wings of wheeling alabaster doves,
    your hands,
Cold and lifeless.
Dropping low against the sweat-stained sheets--like the haunting
    dance of
Ghost-shadows stretching further and further over a barren,
    snow-kissed
Field. And they remember the faint, brisk expulsion of your hot,
    gasping
Breath, garbling on the wind, whispering, even,
As you slipped away,
On time's winged chariot,
And you didn't even say goodbye.

GOOD MORNING

Propped up conveniently on crumpled sections
Of old newspapers,
Twisted and piled in a most precarious pyramid.
The eyes of the blond man are riveted
Upon the old woman.
Bearing down on those filthy rags
He imagined she'd worn since time immemorial.
As always with these people,
These perfidious vagabonds,
He anticipated the piteous mewling,
The tales of woe he knew all too well
To be nothing more than a desperate ruse
Of some scandalous street magician,
Tongue rattling, hands moving furtively
Across the crucible of the eye
In that subliminal flash that can
Only be interpreted as the
Faintest flicker of magic,
Something you knew not to be true
Yet wanted to believe, those sad stories,
Money to ride a chariot to the moon,
Money for hot coffee and a crusty bagel,
Money for parlaying a wicked,
Non-negotiable past into the mundanity
Of three-tiered cakes and
Sweet apple pies, or perhaps,
A soft warm bed,
All those mannequins peeking out
And the cherubic faces of angels
Who appear in the night
Delivering the hot food and warm blankets.
This was the wrought-iron bed
She told them on which she could sleep forever.
This was the place she called home.
She thinks that she'll lose it one day.

She thinks she'll lose it
By mortgage foreclosures, or perhaps
A seizure by some heartless banker.
And she is afraid her lovely home
Will be defenestrated by some
Raving lunatic one night, maybe
During the dead of winter,
And she would be beaten and
Kicked into oblivion.
Weeks later she'll wake up in some cool,
Antiseptic hospital, fightin death-demons,
And finally,
The horde of white-jacketed tormentors
Who'll come to drag her away
To some state-run hospital for crazies,
Where she'd be constantly bombarded
With the shock treatments and
The psychotherapy and the Lithium.
They'll take her so far out,

PHANTOM

And when I'm asleep he constantly creeps, a guardian watching
    over me,
Over evil things,
Lurking in the night,
He, much smaller than you can imagine.
And do not try to touch him--he is intangible--an illusive entity
    that you
Cannot even see on your VCR--he is invisible.
He moves along the blunt edges of my cerebral zones, usurping
    moons,
Distant galaxies, and uninhabited planets. He takes whatever he
    wants, for
He has control.
And I saw him again this morning, there in the bathroom mirror,
His large head and torso visible, pathetically waving his hands;
    he was
Laughing hysterically.
And he talked to me for hours on end.
Though I couldn't understand what he was saying, syllables
    blurred, he
Rambling on in some exotic, lunarian language mute and alien to
    all Mankind.

THE MADMAN SING OF BETTER DAYS

The image of the man
Is only a faint shadow, a sick bag of
Withered bones.
You say when will it ever end?
The ceaseless noise, the desultory rambling,
The hot expulsion of despairing wails,
Cracked, rancid, dry like desert weeds.
You want to believe he'll return one day,
Perhaps to collect his pay--
Just compensation doled out for
The restorations of his faith.
Hidden treasures shimmer in the
Deepest cobalt blue, there,
In the abysmal sea, where he will never
Never rise.
You have to wonder what the man
was like in his youth--
Before the tragic aberration, before the
Schizy interludes, the paroxysmal blues,
Before the unheralded incursion of demons
And the long, grueling days, wracked
His impoverished, bloodless soul like
The agonizing grate of a
Million eerie songs.
The madman sings of better days.
It's the beauty of the moment
That makes you smile, not the hue and mad cries,
Or the quick imaginings of the spectrum too
Bright to see, thoughts too fragmented,
Too real to be true, images,
swarming over the sweat-stained walls
Of his padded cell. It's those songs.
For eighteen harrowing years he's been at it,
Beating his taut, hollow chest,
Drumming the air-bubbles, while singing those

Songs, loud and broken and long forgotten.
All that dust, all that emptiness,
loneliness, all that fire, raging,
Burning, burning.
Railing against God as if He
Were a tangible thing in the sky, as if He
Were some weird silent partner to shake
His fist at, to cavil at,
To hurl stones at.
Oh, Oh, Ba-a-by he sings, *Why did you*
Le-e-ave me? Please, Please come back to me...

DEATH ROW

As if it was a strange biological specimen
straight out of Africa--
the blonde nurse recoils, grimaces, looks away,
She puts on her latex gloves and
a mask to protect herself from this strange
    phenomenon
that has taken heart-throb actors and rock stars
and gay designers whose creations
she now refuses to wear.
So she leans slightly forward
to pick it up--
to whisk it hurriedly to that special ward
for the unrepentant, the cursed, and the damned.
A security clearance is needed to pass through here
The security monitors and the grim-faced
guards toting shotguns and wearing bullet-proof
    vests
Every infant is frisked for weapons, shaken down.
And so the black baby stares up with
glazed, innocent eyes--
punished by the crude histories of
one thousand IV drug abusers and an endless
stream of Bi-sexual lovers.
It feels the cold, impersonal gloved hands
and squints, blinks, confused
as she goes over to the glistening gadgets
and the menacing dark machines that protrude
luminous and veined.
"Prepare for the execution," someone says.
And the infant cries out for its mother
but frail and shrunken and withered
with AIDS--
she died not long ago.

AUTUMN DAWN

And long sleek fingers caress
The autumn dawn, stroke
Erotic heartstrings,
As a tremulous rondeau awakens
The sun,
Its gossamer-orange eyelid rising.
It is where the wind is gentle
beyond the mountainside and
Flocks of birds bathe each morning
In illustrious blue streams winding
Down the valley,
Where weeping mothers place flowers
Beside the gray-blanched stones of dead soldiers.

DARK CITY

You were born in an era
Of great kings and wise teachers,
Who promised you immortality.
Trapped in this urban wasteland
Where the fires rage,
You could see the blood, and
The potent crack-dreams, swarming
amid the dusky haze--
Hovering over the city like
Ghost-shadows--
Over a lost generation--
The heirs to this impoverished doom.
Cold and shallow with
Heartless abandon. You rule your turf
With impunity--homeboys,
To the wild, raucous beat
Of rap music booming from your
Ghetto blasters.
Peddling the poisoned white powder--
Machine guns in your hands--
You strut and preen in the mean,
Lawless streets--
In your state-of-the-art high tops,
Your stylish designer jeans,
Your wet jheri curls,
And your hairless, sweat-drenched
Chest bedecked with bright gold ropes.
And the gargantuan diamond-encrusted
Rings tilled from mines
As distant as your fears
Glimmer faint in the jaundiced eye
Of your sad and tragic future,
as you raise your clenched fist--
Your collective tongues spewing venom
Like a black Mamba rising from

The gray dust--
Invoking the searing death cries
Of gang warfare piercing the air
In the cold, dark city.
And a soft tear falls from
The martyr's eye,
As you begin your carnage.

NAPPY HEADS

Round here is an urban dystopia
Full of nappy ass heads--
Starting where the few black guerrilla
Brigades waged war
On the prestidigitation of the follicles--
Forcing the retro-style hot combs
Into the exile of barren scrapyards--
The pseudo-diplomats
Negotiating the nuclear meltdowns of the
Relaxers and the duke
And the grease-caked jheri-curls.
Martial law is declared on the disgustingly
Long extensions--
And the ridiculous fake weaves are strong
Across a cracker redneck sky
Like the Klu Klux Klowns tight noose in
Billy Holiday's <u>Strange Fruit</u>.
Round here the sistas wear garish colors.
Angela Davis 'fros and tight cornrolls.
The kinks stick up, hand down, swing low.
And the brothas adorn dreads like Marley.
Majestic bushes like Frederick Douglas.
The days streak across a tranquil city
Like a herd of graceful gazelles--
And in the plush quiet funeral parlors--
The caskets are empty.

POSTCARD FROM SOUTH CENTRAL

It was war, G. Anarchy. Rebellion.
Chaos, man--and in it there's no god
Or logic in the hearts and minds of the people--
Cold, oppressed,
Humiliated by the unjust Rodney King verdict,
Which was brutally racist.
It reflected--tragically--the Gulf War.
'member that?
U.S. war planes strafing buildings and homes
In Iraq--
Killing hundreds of innocent women
And children inside them.
I seen it, man. Seen it on TV
So why then was Americans so horrified,
So ticked off by niggahs whippin' that
White boy's ass--what's-his-name?--
Reginald Denny, that's him, on TV
I'll tell you why. Cuz he white.
Cuz a the blood, G. The senseless murders.
The lootin' an' billowing conflagrations'
The fire next time--
Came into every Americans living room,
Unlike the gulf war.
This is what racist Amerikkka caused, B.
This is the mad rage
Peoples subjugated for centuries
can conjure up--
Businesses burnt down, jobs lost,
Peoples kilt, destruction spreading its evil
Tentacles like
Cancer to Korean an' even white businesses
In Beverly Hills!
I was here, man. I seen it. It was crazy.
I seen white folks out there too, G.
Just a lootin' an' killin' an' burning, burnin',

Burnin'!
I guess they was mad too, huh?
Cuz they know African-Americans deserve
Justice an' equality an'
Decent housin' an' education an'
Job opportunities--
Jus' like white folks.

FOR JAMES BALDWIN

And all that was said about
You when you were gone,
The accolades, cascading upon your
bereaved genius.
Did they forget to toss you
The biggest prize of them all?
The crown of glory your big sad
Gentle eyes saw bestowed upon
Lesser gods?
You were angry all the time,
Your beautiful words spewing fires of
Rage leaping from your
Crested boy-preacher past.

PALEST SHADE OF CONFUSION

She was not the palest shade
Of alabaster,
She was not mocha, praline, mahogany,
A cast of bronze or gold
Or some other exotic hue
Her skin was dark, anthracite,
Like a sweet wild blackberry.
Her full heart-shaped lips the color of wine.
The application of concocted creams--
The tinted blue lens over eyes like diamonds
Distorted her distinct African features,
That girl over there, the black girl,
Not her true self at all.
She was not inwardly the virtuous paragon, the
Pretentious façade she thought
Mirrored the traditional all-American look,
The look of the brightest of colors,
Etched into Norman Rockwell painting,
Maybe one with a cute, freckled-face girl,
A little white girl,
With long, blonde pigtails,
There, the little girl in the candy store,
Slouching at the counter,
slurping the fuzzy soda pop.
It was just that everything was so dark,
Slatted drearily, tenebriously dark--
She could only see herself basking
In all that whiteness--
She could only envision wallowing
In those bleached, eurocentric dreams,
Shiny and luminous.
And at that prestigious university
Somewhere in Boston
She did all the things white girls did.
She took the proper major,

Used proper etiquette,
She talked proper,
Never employing black English or dating
Handsome, ebullient dark-skinned boys.
She did nothing antithetical to the
White experience.
She claims she was reared
In the affluent suburbs,
A sweet juicy peach plucked from the bough
Of old-money Bostonians.
Her doting parents were au courant, ardent
Republicans--names gracing the
Social Register--
And she was never around "those people."
Illiterate and black, poor and black,
Slimy, evil and black, listless, jobless,
Promiscuous, syphilitic and black--
Tragically, repulsively--black.
So she circumvents ideals
And agendas not her own--the resolutions,
The hardships and responsibilities, were not
Entirely within her province--the
Afro-American studies,
The sit-ins and the
Non-violent student marches.
Instead, hurling herself into those
Protracted orgies
Where the wide-eyed frat brats
Jerked convulsively to the eerie cackle
Of heavy metal rock music,
As the long-necked glass jugs, glazed and wicked
And bubbly
Clashed violently against giant cool
Metal beer kegs.
And while losing herself in the
Potent sinsemilla clouds
And the crisp white powdered dreams
She tries not to remember

Those sweet sultry lyrics and the
Raucous up-tempo funk playing
Somewhere in the background--
The Whispers singing "chocolate girl."
And James Brown belting out
"I'm black and I'm proud."
Yeah, those slick R & B oldies but
Goodies she pretended not to hear, that she claims
To have no addendum to,
Oh, those songs, she would never
Ever sway her wide hips soulfully to!
It occurred to her that her
Aversion to blackness could be highlighted
With blonde tresses--
Oodles and oodles of it, glowing,
Shimmering in the artificial moonlight--
long dense curtains cascading down.
Turning her head, she moves past
The sign on the shop window--
Strawberry blonde. Platinum blonde.
Dirty blonde. Beach blonde.
Flaxen blonde. Tinged, streaked blonde.
Sun-splashed blonde. Twinkling blue eyes
And blonde. Beautiful, shapely and blonde.
She'd seen the girl on Phil Donahue
She told the clerk--
The girl cut and mortised from
Sleek white marble--You know,
The blonde, what's her name,
That model,
Not the one on the Miss Clairol commercial
But the one on the cover of *Vogue*--
No, no, not the haggard, alcoholic actress,
Not *that* whore, the blowsy thespian,
Her indiscretions splashed across those
Sleazy tabloids--
But the sweet girl-next-door,
Er...what's her name?

And the nervous clerk thinking she
was perhaps some smart lawyer
For the NAACP, maybe even a radical feminist,
Or a covert agent for the Government.
She could be arrested and tried for complicity
Of the act. For the cracking of the
Genetic code. For the illegal cloning of mass confusion.
And so the fidgeting clerk slips
The classified documents from the drawer--
A sense of foreboding swarms her reality--
Handcuff's encircling round her wrist.
Red lights glaring. Cameras clicking.
And she waits to be tossed into some dark cell,
So scary and cold, like those sleeping graveyards
Coveting the dust of Jean Harlow and Marilyn Monroe.

TASHINA

And it all comes back to Tashina on time's winged chariot--
In the hazy glow of neon lights
And the foul supperations washing over her.
--And it all came to her briskly--in the swift heady throes of
    white-powdered dreams
And the swirling visions of hovering uncles and mean sugar
    daddies
Her mama brought home.
Faces black and bronze and sometimes white--
Too imperceptible to put names to.
But she remembered the prurient stares, the nauseous gin-laced
Breath that burned her sweet brown cheeks like Satan's fire.
And the death threats--her silence bribed with sweet hard candy.
"Keep your mouth shut, Lil' girl."
"Sing Tashina."
"Open your tight lil' throat an' blow, you bitch."
Before he can cut it, one said.
Before he kilt her, said another.
Now the cruel, moonless nights ambling down this carnival-like
    strip,
The squalor of seedy motel rooms
And sweet-faced white boys with money to spend.
Of liaisons with catholic nuns out of uniform
And secret nocturnal excursions with black-robed gestapo judges
And horny priests who whispered--
With her long brown legs flung wide--
That she was so dirty and vile and beautiful.

THE HEADLESS CORPSE

Vomit bursting from the rookie's gut--
The detectives and the photographer stood mute and speechless
    in the cold.
Haunting shadows descending into the ravine--
Sliced almost in half by thin, surgical light.
A pen scratched upon paper--
Bulbs flashed--
A wicked gleam upon the battered torso,
Curled in a fetal position in grimy scarlet Victoria Secrets
And fake pink nails clutching the blood-soaked earth.
Who could have done such a thing? What beast or wolf?
Tracing what was left of her--
A farm girl from a small town in Idaho.
A white girl, blonde, cruel and pretentious,
With icy blue eyes full of spangly dreams.
The world was a shit-rich sonuvabitch and she wanted to work
    that sucker.
A magical erotic dream
Whirling in and out of their reality--
She wanted to dance like Madonna,
Like Paula Abdul. She wanted to dance like Ginger and Janet.
One waited. Howled. Stalked.
Another committed suicide.
The last one possessed the swift left hands of a skilled surgeon.
Had to be, the detectives concluded.
Shaking their heads, bagging tissue and fiber for the forensic lab
    boys.
It's the way the heinous operation was performed--
So cold and brutal and precise--
Without the precautionary latex or anesthesia.

PRECIOUS

How many times have I confessed my love for you? Told you
    you're precious--
Like the prospector's find--the rare jewel, obscured beneath the
    matrix.
Passionate fires leaping from my soul-naked crest.
Inner voices muffled by the drone of intimate longings.
Even against the slat of darkness
You shimmer,
Your hair, your eyes, fingertips
Skinny-dipping in undulating waves of invisible light.
And you, your blushing sweetness and tragic shyness--you
    flutter away, like a
Leaf in the wind.
Denying me your soft, lovable qualities, not even affronting
    reality.
You're plain, you say, simple,
Not even beautiful.
Never was, never could be.
But you *are* beautiful, Precious.
And you don't even know it.

WILL I EVER SEE YOU AGAIN?
(FOR ROSIE FEAGINS)

And though I am middle age now
I find myself battling a winter-enlarged midriff.
I find myself constantly worrying about
Heart attacks and strokes.
My hairline has only slightly receded
Yet my hair is still thick and curly and
Shiny and fine.
My eyes are still brown and moist with love.
I am not as handsome as I used to be.
I am still my mother's favorite son.
I still love Tina Marie Songs.
My shambling gait is getting slower
But my mind much quicker.
I am only as superior as yesterday's rain.
My tastes have mellowed to soft jazz
Music and saltless potato chips.
I still smoke those long nasty cigars
And my flash tantrums have alchemized
To harmless bursts of radiant laughter.
I think of you constantly these days
The beauty of you still swims in and
Out of my heart.
Your pictures still hang on my wall.
And we never made love on a bed of roses.
Never swam the rivers on the moon.
And for some inextricable reason I'm still
Madly in love with you.

THE NATURE OF SADNESS

You were there, with him, that night,
And I, with her…four washed-out stars
Orbiting in the space of nothingness.
The others did not seem to have names
    Nor faces.
Meaningless in the shadowy twilight.
And for a fleeting moment our sad eyes met.
Sadness sank in--quickly pirouetted, retreated,
Like precocious dancers.
All that heat between us--
Memories rekindling the passionate flames--
Time taking sharp glances backward--
And then hearts flutter, moans, dies.
Before either of us could speak, a complacent pale
Moon flares like an humongous diamond.
Sinks deep in the howling mouth of a shimmering
Black Atlantic--the wild spray rising like
The avenging ghosts of love's stormy past--
And this night, in muted agony…
We part, once more…

LET'S GET MARRIED

Fidgeting across the table I ponder the
Question: I am not good at this.
Can your ears hear my heart beating
Crazy in my chest?
It's the fear of rejection.
Perhaps you'll say, "It won't work,
We're too young,
Hey, just take a look at the high
Divorce rate in America."
I'll tell you I'm not good at statistics.
We're no longer children pretending to be
Grownups, I'll tell you.
Just think of it: You, lovely in your
White lace, Victorian-style wedding gown,
And me, handsome and proud,
In my rented tux.
A display of family and friends
Will fill the church pews,
A million eyes basking in the
Golden splendor--the prodigious
Floral arrangement--
the silk banners strung across our
Sky--the organ's cool sutra--and
Rice pebbles waiting to fall like
Truffles of white snow.
Locked arm in arm we'll float gingerly
Down the carpeted aisle.
And though I am grinning you can
Feel my knees melting down
Like butter, and the sweat pouring
Down my face.
Perhaps I'm frightened by it all--
What is this thing about taking
The plunge?
Dreamy-eyed, you'll turn to your parents,

Standing there,
Your mother, quietly weeping,
And your stone-faced dad,
Reluctant to give his little girl away.
Your lips will part one last time
To the preacher's litany,
Saying, "Yes, I will",
Taken by your beauty, I'll moan,
"Oh, I do."

DOMESTIC VIOLENCE

And when it was over the wind
Muffled your tears, at dusk,
Blew chills through your heart valves,
Where the glazed ice lay,
There, in the quite cool, tamping down the
Fires in your disapproving gaze.
The mind is an exquisite faculty but I
Will never know unless you talk to me.
Go ahead. Tell me you don't care.
Tell me you dare, you bitch.
Tell me you're sorry that you saw him,
And it came up again,
That eerie feeling, rivers of ecstasy.
It came up through your spatulate toes,
And the kisses reached your wide hips, your spine,
Your lovely breast, quivering, flustered,
Your blood boiling, your head swooning,
That feeling, you said, that rush--
O s-o-o-o good.
It was only a playful nudge. But your
Rubicund cheeks burned a deeper hue,
Your body festooned with sweet-ugly weals
And you were livid with dark despair.
You're such a fragile toy
For the umpteenth time I promise
Not to do it again.
C'mon, it's okay. Give it to me, baby.
Full blasts. Let it go. I can take it.
Let your feminine rage fly through the age of time like mad
      demons with claws
So sharp they cut deep into the flesh,
Into the bones, gimme your best shot--
Go for the eyes--
I love it when you're mad.
Now, wavering in the doorway,

It's a full moon, and there's a
Monstrous leer on your face.
Something glints wicked and cold in
Your small hands--Oh, no!--
Wait a minute, dear! Can't we talk?
I *said* I'll never *do* it again!
Please, put the gun down! Don't shoot!
Oh, God!

THE WAY I SEE HIM

Across the endless coils of shark-teethed razor wire--
over the high stone wall of Babylonia,
and on down the frigid dark corridors
of death row--
Bright orange fingers of the sun
caress the cold, blue steel bars, and in its
crucible a warmth slowly reveals
the mystery of the Creator

That's the Way I See Him.

In the fathoms of a blue sky,
In the helixes of a green earth, and in the
shimmers of pink and burst
of a magenta moon--He is not a painting
splayed across the sweat-stained canvas
of the wall--
nor a mirage, visible or invisible,
seen or unseen, wavering in and out of my cold reality.

He's my Homeboy, a Presence beyond my shoulder,
when the wicked convict plots,
when the guard's evil glare cuts through stone,
and when death's infinite hand looms,
he is there, yeah, over there.

In the twinkle of a child's sweet angelic eyes,
on the swift wings of pleasant dreams
carried in the night--
and even in the kind and compassionate
words of the Christians who write
to me--a castaway, the wretched, and
the condemned--

That's the Way I See Him

ON THE DAY THE CHILDREN MARCHED
(For the Bruder hof Children's Crusade To Death Row--
August 18-20, 1997)

On the day you marched they said the angels
were with you,
Winding through New Meadow Run and on
Down the highways, trouncing across
Inauspicious redneck counties and
Into buildings where God reigned.

Heading towards Babylon--braving the
Wind and the rain and satan's fire--
You didn't come because of some
Twisted notion of heroism,
You weren't drawn by romantic visions
Of martyrdom or self-aggrandizement.
The thing is, you could have been anywhere--
Wallowing in the decadent playgrounds
        of indifference,
Lolling in the murky dark shadows
Of blissful ignorance, yeah,
Safe and secure behind your impenetrable
Fortress of hypocrisy and indignation.

On the day you marched God smiled down
        on you--
Because you see an injustice and
You want to correct it.
You see racism and you want to cure it,
And you see the brutal inequity of
Capitol punishment and you want to abolish it.

THE SPIRIT OF ANGELS

Seemingly every twenty years or more,
There's a gargantuan event that stirs the
Collective conscientiousness--
An occurrence galvanizing a mass movement,
Something that melts the hardest of hearts,
And loosens the chains that binds
The spirit of goodness.
That something is the Children's Crusade
To death row.

FOR THE JUNIORS FOR JUSTICE

You are our children,
Our brothers and sisters.
Our little, beautiful babies.

You're my friends, too.
The gang.
The award-winning cast of my play.

You couldn't have known that you're all
My personal angels,
    God appointed.

FOR AMEENAH

Death row took me so far out,
Far, far away--
And I never got to see you blossom.
Jennifer claims you're mine, my daughter,
My baby girl, my beautiful little princess,
And I would never deny it. <u>You</u> <u>are</u>.
Tommy and Fats and Charlie and the
Rest of my old gang says the same thing--
"Boy, she looks just like you!" Proud and regal
With your shiny curly hair and plum-colored
Lips--the DNA wouldn't even matter--because
I'll leave the world to you.

PERMANENT PLAYBACK

Clicking back, the best things
Are preserved in the memories of daylight.
'Round 1968 they killed the dreamer--and
I was a young buck caught up in the riots.
'Round 1972-'73, I sang in a band, imitating
Stevie. Then came my hustlin' days.
Supa dupa fly. The return of the mack.
Yeah, sweet sweet back.
"The black man is gawd, brotha! An' the
White man is the devil!" Someone in the
Nation of Islam screamed at me in '75.
In my crisp, sharp-pressed F.O.I. uniform
And black horn-rims--
You couldn't tell me I wasn't the reincarnation
Of Malcolm.
Up in Rahway State Prison in 1978, someone
Said, "Boy, you look like a young Joe Louis",
And next thing you knew I was
The welterweight champ, knocking suckers out.
You could fall in love with old
Black and white movies.
In the ghetto, I thought I was Cagney.

KISSING JOSEPHINE

Death fleets past the midnight train
Heading towards Paris--through the Latin quarter,
Into the dark jazz club near the Seine,
Coltrane blows and "Pops" Armstrong sings,
While Lady Holliday and Miles argue passionately.
The smoke swirls and ebbs about
The murky interior like ghost-shadows waltzing.
I see Baldwin and Wright and Ellison
In a corner harping about books. At the
Bar, Marilyn slaps Hemingway.
Cab Calloway dances circles around Ella.
More! More Vin Rouge for The Black Expatriate!
Scott Fitzgerald yells, Romancing Dandridge
At a table by the stage--
I see Dubois kissing Josephine.

ONE DAY SOON

One day soon heaven will descend the rains
Upon the dry sands of Ethiopia
Sprouting the nurtured seed
Replenishing a once-proud people
Their earthly needs.
Beautiful brown bodies now ugly shrunken shells
Dehydrated skin, big bulging eyes, empty
Stomachs swelled
I cry
I cry
Sometimes late at night
Asking the Lord
Why?
Why are they suffering this terrible plight?
They deserve not crumbs meant for dogs
Nor the many lies of deceit
But a feast of joy
Not scams from scoundrels using them
For their financial ploys
Come oh angels
Cascade the manna in milky streams
Let them feast
Send the rains
Help them restore the lost kingdom
Of their dreams.

WHISPERS

And whispers soothing my ears like
The erotic gentle touch
Of massaging hands.
Like the rush of the wind
As it beats against the grass.
I hear whispers--sweet whispers,
Quiet, smooth and soft.
The landing of dust
In Grandmother's loft.
Listen to your heartbeat.
Can you hear it in the night? Or falling
Autumn leaves tumbling in flight?
And thy parted lips which tongue
That blows,
That sweet placid sound like flakes of
Windswept snow.
A delicate rhythm, a cool quiet swirl,
A faint distant cry in the night,
Of a young brokenhearted girl.

ANTIQUITY

At that moment the drum rolled,
The guitar wept, horns blazed--
The piano's keys ebbed and flowed
To the sultry jazz cut.
Diamonds twinkling.
Her hair coifed, glazed,
Deep anthracite eyes set wide
In mocha sheets beneath her sequin gown--
Cleavage flashing in and out.
She slinks across the floodlit stage--
Moving with the graceful
Feline ease of a cat--
Long, sleek legs striding through
Some exotic dream
That you fell through-that you're
Held captive to--
Lena.
And at the song's end the air
Exploded with ringing applause--
The bouquet of roses falling
From the starlit sky
As long dense curtains tumbled down--muffling
The roar--rippling over this ageless beauty--
And the crowd left holding the dream.

BROWN EYES

Sparkling brown eyes
Chestnut pearls
Vicissitudes of light
Sometimes golden, sometimes bronze
A classical beauty, such a pretty girl
What you see could very well be variegation
Crowds gathering about to study this
Subject of fascination
Bright eyes bright
A story yet to unfold
A *son et lumiere*, a spectacle to behold!
Magical eyes flashing a magician's grand illusion
Cat eyes luminescent in hazel darkness
Like creeping intrusions
Mysterious eyes picking you apart
Evil eyes glaring at jealous hearts
For no man can possess her
She belongs to the world
What a spoiled scarlet beauty, such a pretty girl
A jeweler's delight, a twinkling sprite
Her brown eyes innocent, alluring, magnificent bright…
Ah, but what you see could be a wicked tool
A sweet glowing trap!
A seduction for fools!!!!

WHISPER I'M GONE

Till the sad, sad songs from the trumpet player
Fades into the distance.
Till the last tears tumble upon my grave.
Show them the pictures of memories when I was
Young, handsome and tall.
My matinee smile was just an extension,
For I was a man of class,
Of true distinction.
Kiss goodbye the many beautiful women
That were crazy for me.
Say that I was gallant. Of honor.
A goodman with no intentions of leaving
Them in misery.
Make them forgive me for the debts I left behind,
The alimony checks, the precious spilled wine…
But let them fight.
Let them curse my name in disgrace.
And let them scowl.
Let them kick dirt in my face.
But let the girls cry and say goodbye….
Till the slithering eel returns with the tide;
Till the dust of my body blows far and wide.
No prodigious arrangements should be made off hand;
No loud talking preachers,
Or glittering caskets,
No sad faces veiled behind black,
Or flowers laden in big white baskets.
Just a hush, or a whisper,
Or a sweet mellow song,
Is merely enough
To say that I am gone.
Please tell mother that I went out like a soldier.
Tell her to shed no tears.
And tell grandmother I'll forever miss her,
To the enemies! Tell them it's really been fun.

I had one hell of a laugh.
Of tricks, of sin.
A sexual bash!
Only diamonds are forever.
Oh, how I wish I could stay.
Say that I departed this life,
That I quickly slipped away...

QUEENS RISE
(For the Women on Death Row)

They've stolen your crown, Crestfallen and Broken.
Your sheer majesty snatched from
Society's pristine womb.
But remember this;
Faith liberated Jonah from the
Belly of the beast.

The light of your sweet smile
Has long faded--
But you're still beautiful.
Laughter still glimmers in the depths
Of your tortured eyes.
Your mail was slow this week.
But please don't think you're forgotten.

Perched atop endless islands
Of glistening razor wire
And cold stone ledges--
Melodic bird songs carry messages
Of hope and glad tidings.
They lower their wings in mercy.
The night stars act as your angelic escorts.

You go back through the lineage of Queens--
To Sheba, Ester, Cleopatra, Elizabeth,
And La-ti-fah.

SHANIQUA IS PREGNANT

Now that he has fouled her with his suppurations and a
    monstrosity
Protrudes from her sweet brown hips
That no longer taste like candy--
Dante says: "You jockin' my groove, Bitch,"
And split with the same lame-ass excuse used to doff Tonia and
    the twins.

Shaniqua counts the days on swollen fingers--
Remembering those hot nights awashed
In his funky-ass-sweat--
Wishing she'd listened to her Mama's stories
About nasty boys and full-grown lips
And those oldies-but-no-damn-goodies.

"You gotta git rid of it, Shaniqua," her Mama says. "You only
    14."
"No I ain't. Uh-Uh. Naw. This is _my_ damn baby," She says.
"I ain't killin' it. I ain't no supporter of the death penalty."

She wanted a boy with big ass dreams and wings like Michael
    Jordan.
She'd get to go to places young Black girls ain't neva seen;
Hollywood. Paris. Disney world.
She ain't had a damn penny for pampers or baby clothes
Or even a decent crib but two things for sho' she'll give him
Is a bunch of luv and a good name--
She was already thinking about something close enough
To greatness and far from this trifling-ass Ghetto.

JOHNNY'S A PAINTER

They made him begin again
With childhood scrawls of an uncle's
Nasty genitalia that emerged years later
As impastoed striations of genius.
In deft strokes of abstract vignettes
And tormented <u>Portraitures</u>
You could still see the beautiful mosaic
Of Johnny's Smile--the shimmering
Dreamscapes splattered across the canvas
Of his eyes,
Luminous and colorful.
When he was well enough
They moved him to the hollowed-out cell
With the sun-bleached white walls like an asylum.
This was where Picasso's mistress
Commingled in the array of exotic
Sleeping angels hung as if from
Gauguin's heaven.

WHAT I NEED

At my age I don't need much.
I can get by on beans and biscuits.
Maybe a Lil' slice of apple pie on the side.
Gimme a sweet fat girl.
One who ain't got ten baad ass kids.
One or two, to holler at.
And leave me the hella 'lone in my shack way out.
A Satellite dish.
A Coltrane CD.
And an old, beat up Mustang to get around in.
I been gone too damn long.
Kick me back. Back to the streets.
Puh-leeze. Lemme make parole.
At my age I don't need much.

I can get by on beans and biscuits.

WEST OF INDIA

It could've been an exotic dream that I found myself
    Among the tribes.
Or maybe it was the blood red memories of long dead
    Warriors.
Long after the extermination and the diseases and the
Desecration of the sacred ghosts--
What's left is the scattered proud remnants Custer's punk ass
    Couldn't touch,
The toxins have poisoned their land--
But a single drop of the whites man's firewater
Roiling through generations hasn't deterred the dream--
not when the circle can be restored.

The Indian tribal youth still respect the elders,
They still hold the tradition of the language of the
    Ancestors,
But most of all--they still dance the jingle.

IN THE VALLEY OF THE PROPHETS

Somewhere in Iraq and past Bosnia on through
Tiny war torn villages in Yugoslavia Gabriel's army of Angels
March across a blood-red sky--
And Satan flees on his coward's wings.
Bombs melt into harmless oblivion of a sacred Sun over Kosovo,
And death is an impatient watcher on doorsteps.
They told them the Angel of the mountains pirouettes
To the beat of the wind--
And flocks of pink and blue-streaked swans splash about in
    golden ponds.
There is a promise of no sadness or pain or hunger here.
The crisp clean rivers spills out sustenance.
Infants carillon-like giggles lilt sweetly
On the vestered air and soars across the valley,
Where butterflies flutter about and form exotic halos
Above the worshippers who prostrate in the slatted shadows
Of the Holy Prophets, some they slayed,
Others whose stories are just too painful to tell.
Flowers bloom atop the mass graves nurtured by the
Tears of Muslim women.
"But you don't have to worry," the Recording angel tells them.
"You don't have to cry."
Because he is the All-Hearing, the All-Seeing--
He hears the prayers of every suppliant
With the morning symphony of Solomon's birds.

SAD STORIES ARE ALWAYS TRUE

Among, the tortures and devastations of life is this then--our friends are not able to finish their stories. (Virginia Woolf--The Waves, 1931)

It took the ink of vast oceans and the assembly of writing angels
to
Record these stories.
Dust-Motes floats like silent ghosts
From the pages now--crinkled and frayed at the edges.
Old slave bones chained in the cool deep of the Passage,
See all those Jews aflame in ovens,
And the contorted brown faces strung taut by the terror of the
noose.
Retching in vomit, sprawled naked on bathroom floors,
Lolled in the permanent drift of a midnight sleep.
The angels arranged the names in no particular order:
Lenny Bruce.
                                        Dorothy Dandridge
                    Jimmie Hendricks
                                        Billie Holliday.
Janice Joplin.

Cats like the Yardbird and Coltrane and Miles left on three blasts
Of Israfil's Trumpet--
But you'll need wings to fly through the Pharaoh's dreams.
There's the lost Epistles of John Brown.
A final Chapter on Malcolm's reunion with Sista Betty.
Lady Di shimmers on the same glossy page as Tupac and
Princess Grace
And Biggie Smalls.
Flip through the timeless drama of the Rosenbergs and the
Kennedy's and that dreamer,
Martin, beautifully weaved.

The unnamed soldiers pose in elegant battle regalia are given

Names and ranks. And if you go there--(And this brilliant prose,
    too)
The section called "The Tormented Writers", and infinite queue,
Where you'll find me, myself, among the tragic Poets.

FLOWERS FOR OLD SMOKEY

They only wanted to hear the nasty tales from his dark days--
It didn't matter that they said they loved him.
Legend has it he'd knocked out plenty suckers as a wild young
    buck.
Done a straight 45 year bit.
Now his old eyes are weary and wrinkled and
Tear-streaked at the corners.
Claims it comes from witnessing the horrors of three lifetimes.
They should've let him go when the
Wind strikes his sail and wings of wisdom sprout.
Black dreams are buried deep in this concrete hell.
Let him rest in peace.

FOR RONALD O'SHEA

I remember when you came to Death Row in 1987. A burly Irish
    guy from the rough side of Pittsburgh.
You had quick wits, and effectuous sense of humor, and a gentle
    disposition that
confounded any cruel Prosecutors' image portraying you as
    some heartless beast that
should be put to death.
I never bothered to ask you what the Catholic Faith taught about
    forgiveness, or Pat
O'Brien or James Cagney in <u>Angels With Dirty Faces</u>, or if you
    ever wore green on Saint
Patrick's Day.
But I did know you, O'shea. I was afforded lingering glimpses
    into the purity of your
heart, the laudable deeds of your soul, I heard your jolly laughter
    that shook death row as
if it rumbled up from some plateau of goodness.
In recent years, a series of inextricable diseases and phantom
    afflictions dogged you,
man. I watched helplessly as your quick powerful gait became a
    slow torturous struggle.
"Yo, O'shea!" I'd holler at you whenever I saw you shuffling in
    and out of the Doctor's
office. "You better get my money!"
"What money? I don't owe you any money, Reggie."
"Find out when I catch you, Chump".
"Yeah, right", you'd reply painfully, flashing a 100 watt smile.
And remember the times I'd pretended we had a beef in the yard-
    -and we'd sparred
playfully? For a sickly old head you still had a vicious left hook.
This winter, a nasty strain of the Flu blew across the U.S. and on
    through death row with
a fury.
One morning, I heard that the guards found you dead in your
    cell.

In a sick way I would have tried to revive you with laughter.
I might have shouted "Just hold on! Hold on, you old fart! Cuz
   you still owe me money!"
But I guess the last laugh was on you.

MEN DO CRY

You can see it in their bravado, in the intimidating glares and the
    exaggerated swagger
and the nasty brown mounds jammed between pink pitbull jowls.
Glimpses of damaged Psyches--
Wacked out ex Marines--
This is not just a job but an adventure.
You can imagine them getting the drill:
Great day today.
But shooting range Black dummies ain't the feel of the real
    thing, you know, beating
down <u>baad</u>ass niggas
And po' ass white men--the ones who couldn't <u>Knock On Any</u>
    <u>Door</u>.
They never had much anyway.
They took what was left on a shakedown.
Death row teems with sad, broken, hungry men.
Some mornings they serve cold coffee for breakfast.
Late at night Black radio wails those tragic love songs.
When no one seen us--
We sip hot tears.

SACRED WRIT
(FOR KATHY SWEDLOW, ESQUIRE, AND ERIC ON THEIR WEDDING DAY)

If this is the end of my boyish flirtations and your stern
    admonishments during legal
visits.
If this signals the finality of your giggles behind
the glass at my raunchy bedroom jokes--
or you fleeing my roving eye, or words ordinarily reserved for
    spinsters.
Out of respect, then, decorum and etiquette,
for the newly married.

But this is a claim you never raised, Counselor.
Hoping this isn't some fly-by-night Vegas shotgun wedding--
at least a three-tiered cake and wine and greasy chicken wings.

Eric has to be one helluva guy.
To negotiate this sacred Writ.
To have snared this brilliant Legal Strategist.
To rein in, Pin down, break in,
this bucking Courtroom Stallion.

In case you didn't know, Homie. Rumor has She's withered
baad ass Prosecutors with just one look.
Brow beat down a few Masochistic Judges.
Went toe-to-toe with some of the best expensive mouthpieces.

Maybe an even brighter gleam will leap into her
Daddy's eyes. Maybe this will get her Mama to thinkin' (again)
about Grandbabies, perhaps another little Kathy,
some argumentative, brief writing brat,
or a bright Eric, Jr.

If marriage will make you an even better Lawyer--

If it contributes to getting me off Death Row--
then <u>you</u> say, Hell Yeah, you damn right--<u>I Do.</u>

BORDER CROSSINGS

(For Patricia Jean Rovensky and the Canadian Coalition against
the Death Penalty)

They remember you as the sweet girl from the Republic of South
    Africa,
bright-eyed and festooned in prayer beads
and clutching rosaries and the dreams of a better tomorrow.
They say that even Nelson Mandela remembers you--
The Platinum blond now a full-fledged woman
with the heart and soul of the weeping Black Madonna--
and who became an outspoken opponent against Apartheid.

You're Canadian royalty to me. Yes you is.
A fierce Activist.
Wounded Sista-Soldier-Friend.
Tough enough to spar with Ruben "Hurricane" Carter.

You'd bring down baad ass Dictators,
wicked Municipalities,
Corrupt Politicians and Judges--
release the captives, set the caged birds free,
yes you would.

Even amid blinking screens and laboratory test tubes
and your morning lectures--
you still find time to wing through cyberspace,
a merciful Angel seeking Justice.
CROSSING BORDERS,
onto foreign soil--
and into the dark Death Rows of Amerikkka.

IF I AM SUCH A GOOD WRITER

Then why do the hearts of men rage,
mouths twist and foam like rabid dogs--
the spittle that flies when they speak my name,
curse my flame,
call me every-damn-thang,
but the Man my Daddy made me?

Yet it's said compare my style
to Jimmy Baldwin, Richard Wright,
Ralph Ellison and even Langston Hughes--
True, I was the little brown boy
who shined his shoes,
up in Harlem.

I hear ghost voices of those cool black cats--
jazz baby, guiding my pen seep sop seep sopping
blood-red poems screaming through a death row midnight--
while they plot and scheme evil things,
clip snip clip my wings--
they can only dream that I die tomorrow.

About the Author

Reginald S. Lewis is an African-American poet, essayist and playwright on death row in Waynesburg, Pennsylvania. His poems, essays and stories have appeared in numerous periodicals in the United States, Canada and England. He has garnered several writing awards for his work, including three awards in P.E.N. American Center (writing awards for prisoners). Two of his plays have been professionally produced. His deep concern for the well being of troubled young people has earned him the respect and admiration of many.